NOV

S is for the Stanley Cup

A Hockey Championship Alphabet

Written by Mike Ulmer and Illustrated by Chris Lyons

Hockey players all around the world know the Stanley Cup is the hardest trophy to win in professional sports. After an exhausting 82-game schedule, a team must battle through four playoff rounds and as many as 28 games before the winning captain is handed the Cup.

Raising the Cup into the air is the ultimate moment for a player and a franchise. The sight of a captain lifting the Cup is so inspiring, hometown spectators usually stay, applaud, and watch when the visiting team is awarded the trophy.

The first thing players do when given the Cup
is lift it and lift it and lift it straight up.
And from hand to hand it is passed and shared,
given a kiss and raised back in the air.

B is for Baptism

A tender child will never know
that water flowed into a silver bowl
and that their name was given when
the Cup was placed right under them.

It turns out that having a trophy with a bowl on top can be pretty handy. Colorado Avalanche defenceman Sylvain Lefebvre and his wife had their daughter baptized in the Cup in 1996. A Swedish cousin of Detroit's Tomas Holmstrom borrowed the Cup and used it to baptize his baby in 2008.

The Cup itself was baptized in a different way in the 1960s when Toronto's Red Kelly put his baby son Conn in it. Being a baby, Conn did not know he was not supposed to pee in the Stanley Cup. Don't worry. They washed it very thoroughly.

When it was originally presented in 1893 the Cup was just a silver bowl attached to a wooden pedestal.

Unlike many other trophies, the Stanley Cup bears the names of nearly every player or team executive to win it. In 1924 the Montreal Canadiens began the formal tradition of including a new ring with the players' names every year. The Cup became so large it came to be known as "the Elephant Leg" or "the Stovepipe." The Cup was redesigned in 1958 with five rings containing the names of 13 teams per ring.

To be eligible for inclusion a player needs to have played half his team's regular season games or at least one playoff game. Another fun fact: the members of the winning team are allowed to borrow the Cup for one day.

C is for Cup

It takes about a pound of weight
per inch of silver atop the plate.
It's just short of three feet high
and in pounds, just under 35.

D is for the Dawson City Nuggets

By dogsled, train, and bike they roamed.
They must have worried they'd never get home.
They crossed 4,000 miles of lonely terrain,
lost two games and went home again.

D d

During hockey's early days, any team could challenge for the Cup. In 1904 the Dawson City Nuggets undertook the most difficult road trip in history. They travelled by foot, bicycle, dog-sled, boat, and train from their Yukon mining town to Ottawa where they met the Ottawa Silver Seven. It took the Yukoners 24 days to reach the capital but they were only given one day to rest and were outscored 32–4 by the home side over the two games.

The Nuggets played several exhibition games on the way home but never challenged for another Cup.

E e

E is for Events

Trouble was sometimes close behind
when the Cup was taken for a ride.
Today it's treated with the greatest care
and not forgotten anywhere.

After working so hard to win it, players can be very careless with the Stanley Cup. According to Cup legend, members of the victorious 1905 Ottawa Silver Seven tried to drop-kick the Cup over Ottawa's frozen Rideau Canal. The Cup was recovered the next day. In 1924, members of the Montreal Canadiens were en route to a party when their car had a flat. They put the Cup at the side of the road while they fixed the tire. The players forgot the Cup and had to retrace their steps to recover it.

Today the Cup always travels with an official from the Hockey Hall of Fame to make sure it is handled carefully.

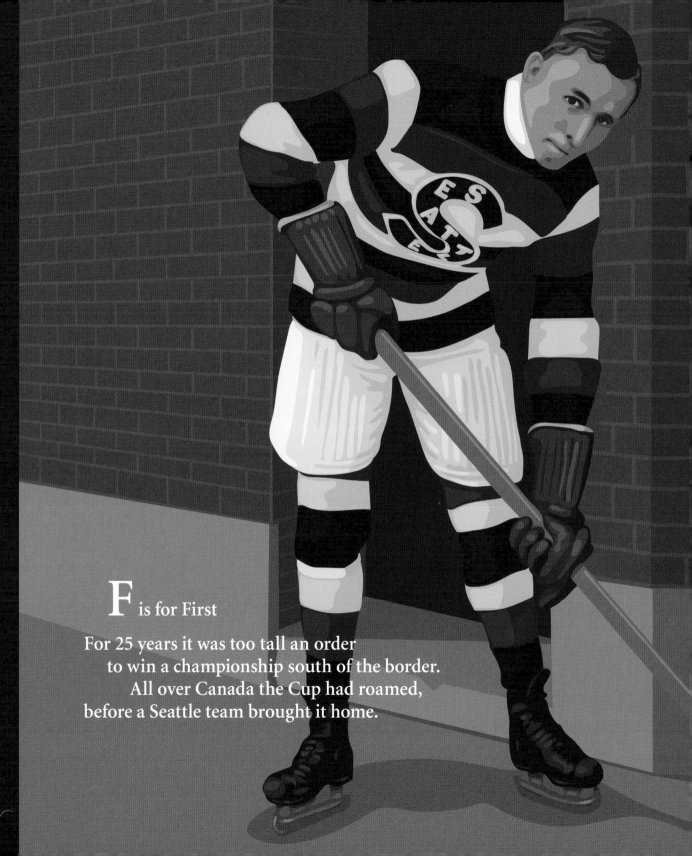

The Seattle Metropolitans became the first American team to win the Stanley Cup when they beat the Montreal Canadiens three games to one in 1917. That trip across the border would be the first of countless journeys to cities all over the world. Peter Forsberg became the first player to take the Stanley Cup to Europe when he brought it to his Swedish hometown in 1996. The Cup was taken to Moscow's Red Square in 1997.

The Stanley Cup has travelled farther than any championship trophy and has been welcomed to the White House by five presidents.

F f

F is for First

For 25 years it was too tall an order
to win a championship south of the border.
All over Canada the Cup had roamed,
before a Seattle team brought it home.

G is for Good Luck

There're lots of things you must repeat
    if your team is on a winning streak.
That battered stick, a favourite puck
    are golden if they bring good luck.

Hockey players are a superstitious bunch and even the best players must sometimes sacrifice to keep a good-luck charm in place.

In 1959 a low-scoring Montreal Canadiens player named Marcel Bonin needed a pair of gloves and started using those belonging to teammate Maurice "Rocket" Richard after the great star was injured. Bonin, who had never before scored in 25 playoff games, fired 10 goals in just 11 postseason contests. When "the Rocket" returned from his injury all his teammates said Bonin should continue to wear the lucky gloves. It worked. Bonin scored two goals against Toronto in the final and the Canadiens won the Cup.

H h

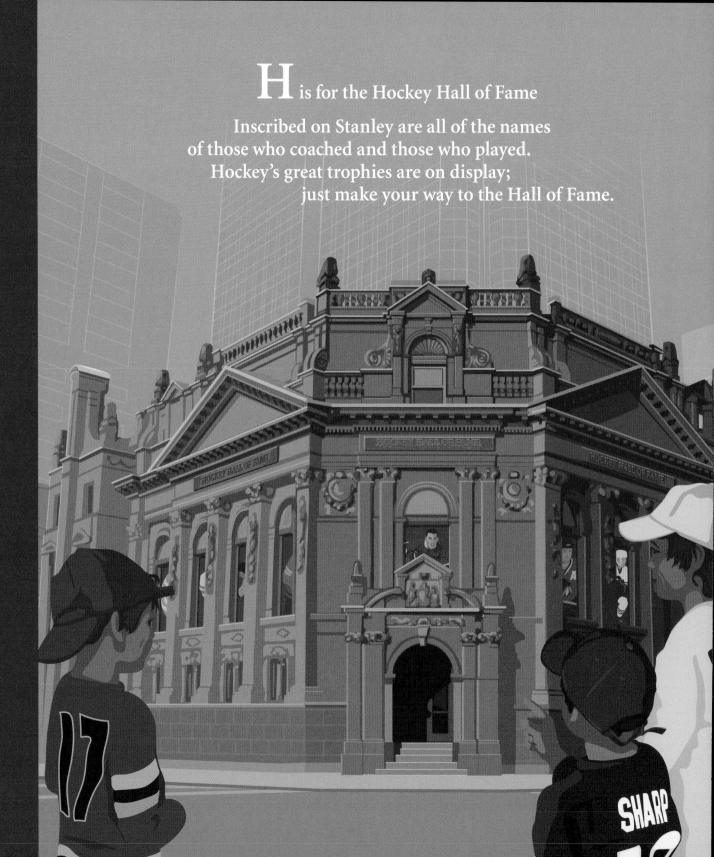

H is for the Hockey Hall of Fame

Inscribed on Stanley are all of the names
of those who coached and those who played.
Hockey's great trophies are on display;
just make your way to the Hall of Fame.

The Hockey Hall of Fame in downtown Toronto is the home of the Stanley Cup. You will also find artifacts and exhibits that touch on every element of hockey's evolution in Canada, the United States, and Europe. Induction into the Hall is the highest honour a player, official, or team executive can earn. When the Presentation Cup is on the road, a replica Cup is on display.

Each year 300,000 people visit the Hall.

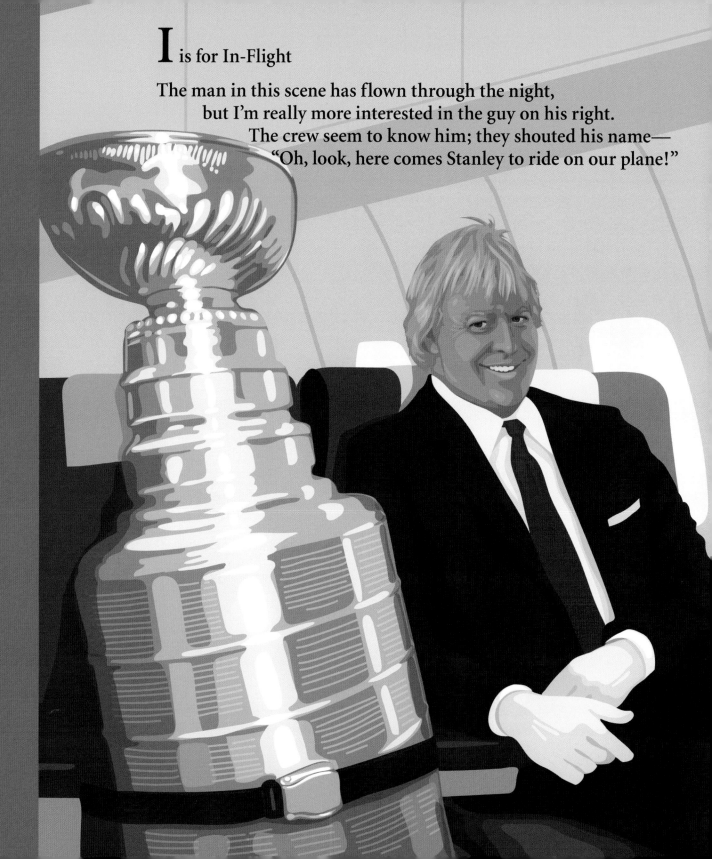

Phil Pritchard, the curator of the Hockey Hall of Fame, has been photographed with the Stanley Cup more than anyone on the planet. While usually kept in a custom case, the Cup is sometimes given a first-class seat of its own beside Pritchard. If you look closely, you will notice the white cotton gloves Pritchard uses whenever he handles the Cup. The gloves help to keep the trophy smudge-free.

The Cup has travelled countless miles across Canada, the United States, the Czech Republic, Sweden, Norway, Russia, Slovakia, and many more countries. Whenever they travel with the Cup, Pritchard and the rest of the team from the Hall of Fame add in extra time so the people who handle the Cup—customs officials, airline people—as well as passengers can have their pictures taken with it.

I is for In-Flight

The man in this scene has flown through the night,
but I'm really more interested in the guy on his right.
The crew seem to know him; they shouted his name—
"Oh, look, here comes Stanley to ride on our plane!"

I i

J is for Jacques Plante, King of the Goalies

His last name was Plante; his first name was Jacques,
a goalie best known for his game-changing stops.
It was true back then and it's still true today:
you don't win a Cup if you don't get the saves.

J j

Goalies and hockey fans owe a great debt to goaltending genius Jacques Plante, who won six Stanley Cups with the Montreal Canadiens. Plante is credited with inventing the goalie mask and was the first goalie to leave his crease to field loose pucks.

Patrick Roy, who tended goal for the Canadiens and the Colorado Avalanche, is the only player to win the Conn Smythe Trophy as the playoff's most valuable player three times. The award is named after Conn Smythe, the founder of the Toronto Maple Leafs.

K is for Kenora

It wasn't for long but still it's a fact
the Thistles of Kenora were Stanley Cup champs.
So scoff if you like at their shortened Cup run
but few are the cities to even win one.

THE KENORA THISTLES
1907

In January, 1907, a hockey team from Kenora, comprising
E. Giroux (goal).   A. H. Ross (point).
S.I. Griffis (cover point).   T. Hooper (rover).
W. McGimsie (centre)   R.Beaudro (right wing).
and T. Phillips (captain and left wing).
defeated the Montreal Wanderers in two challenge games
at Montreal to win the Stanley Cup. The team was
coached and trained by J. A. Link. The trophy, emblematic
of the Canadian championship, had been presented by
the Governor General, Baron Stanley of Preston in 1892.
Kenora is the smallest town ever to win the Cup.
Erected by the Ontario Archaeological and Historic Sites Board.

Kenora, Ontario, present population 15,000, is the smallest Stanley Cup–winning city. The 1907 Thistles beat the Montreal Wanderers in two straight games to win the Cup, but two months later the Wanderers regained the trophy in a rematch.

Like the Thistles, several teams named on the Cup no longer exist. The Ottawa Silver Seven, Quebec Bulldogs, Seattle Metropolitans, and Winnipeg Victorias also took home the trophy.

To reach the Stanley Cup final but fall short is always painful for fans and players but it is even more heartbreaking when the loss comes in the final game of the best-of-seven series. Just ask the Vancouver Canucks who were beaten by Boston in 2011. The 2008–09 Red Wings seemed seconds away from tying their Game 7 in the final moments when Penguins goalie Marc-André Fleury slid across the crease to stop Nicklas Lidström and gain the Cup for Pittsburgh.

Buffalo Sabres fans still talk about the team's loss in Game 6 of the 1999 final because Brett Hull, who scored the winner for the Dallas Stars, had a part of his skate in the crease. Officials ruled the goal was valid.

L is for Losses

Quite often the tears will flow from the winner
and splash on the names carved into the silver.
But sometimes the losers can't help but tear up
while watching their rivals skate around with the Cup.

L1

M m

M is for Mark Messier

Score is what he had to do
to make his victory promise true.
First one, then two, then number three—
His hat trick came with a guarantee.

Mark Messier scored the winning goal as the 1993–94 New York Rangers won their first Cup in 54 years by defeating the Vancouver Canucks in seven games. A few weeks before, in the Eastern Conference Final against New Jersey, Messier guaranteed a Rangers win. With the team down three games to two, Messier predicted the Rangers would win in New Jersey to force a Game 7. "We know we have to win. We can win it and we are going to win it," he told reporters. With the Rangers trailing 2–0, Messier set up a goal and scored three more to lead the Rangers to a 4–2 win.

N is for Marguerite Norris

She liked to give out little gifts;
her quiet words made spirits lift.
And so in hockey progress came
when the Cup displayed a woman's name.

N
n

Marguerite Norris inherited the Detroit Red Wings from her father, Jim, in 1952. She soon became a favourite of her players, who appreciated her kindness and concern for their welfare. As president of the Red Wings, she became the first woman to have her name on the Cup when the Wings won the trophy in 1954. Fourteen more women would follow, including Sonia Scurfield who won the Cup in 1989 as co-owner of the Calgary Flames.

While there are many father/son combinations on the Cup there is one notable mother/son set. Charlotte Grahame, an executive with the Colorado Avalanche, saw her name included on the Cup in 2001. Three years later, her son John, a backup goalie for the Tampa Bay Lightning, won the Cup.

O is for Octopus

Two guys decided what the Red Wings needed
was a reminder of going undefeated.
Just win four straight, then do it twice:
but oh, the smell when it hit the ice.

Tossing an octopus onto the ice in Detroit is probably hockey's oddest tradition. It began in 1952 with two brothers, Pete and Jerry Cusimano. The Red Wings were one game away from winning the Cup in the minimum eight games. The brothers owned a fish market and decided that an octopus, with its eight arms, would be the perfect symbol for eight wins. They heaved it onto the ice, the Wings won the next game, and a new tradition was born.

The octopi come out each year the Red Wings make the playoffs. The Wings even keep a huge mock octopus in the wings of the Joe Louis Arena.

Nashville Predators fans got into the act when they tossed catfish onto the ice in the Stanley Cup finals against the Pittsburgh Penguins.

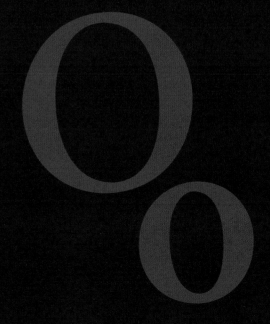

Pp

P is for Presentation Cup

There's one Cup usually on display
and one that's always locked away.
The Presentation Cup is the one they say
goes rather well with champagne.

So how many Stanley Cups are there? That's not as simple a question as you might think.

The original Cup, the one donated by Lord Stanley (see Letter S), was secretly replaced in the late sixties because it was becoming brittle with age. The Presentation Cup, the one given to members of each championship team, is on display at the Hockey Hall of Fame. When the Presentation Cup is on the road, an identical replica is on hand for visitors to the Hall.

The Montreal Canadiens have won the Stanley Cup a record 24 times. Former captain Henri Richard holds the record for Stanley Cup wins by a player with 11. Because he also worked as a team executive, Jean Béliveau's name appears on the Cup 17 times, including ten times as a player. The Canadiens have given the game a long parade of superstars, including Howie Morenz; the Richard brothers, Henri and Maurice; Jacques Plante; Ken Dryden; Yvan Cournoyer; Guy Lafleur; and Patrick Roy.

Montreal has a special place in hockey history. It is where the National Hockey League was established on November 26, 1917. The original NHL teams were the Montreal Canadiens, Montreal Wanderers, Ottawa Senators, and Toronto Arenas.

Q is for Quebec, Home of the Montreal Canadiens

For 23 years they were the top of the heap
and the Cup was paraded down Montreal streets.
Now Canadiens' fans from East Coast to West
await Stanley's return to the place it knows best.

R is for Records

It's fine to study, good to find
which player did most with the Cup on the line.
But take my advice, save yourself time—
Keep counting until you hit 99.

Wayne Gretzky holds current records for playoff goals (122), playoff assists (260), playoff points (382), points in one playoff (47 over 18 games), and three or more goal games (10). Wayne wore two nines as a tribute to his hero, Gordie Howe (fondly called Mr. Hockey), who held many of the regular-season records Wayne broke. As the league's all-time leading scorer, it makes perfect sense that Wayne was selected to serve as the official ambassador for the National Hockey League's centennial celebration in 2017.

Chris Chelios, a defenceman who starred in Montreal, Chicago, and Detroit, holds the record for playoff games played with 266.

As for Stanley Cup wins by a coach . . . that record belongs to Scotty Bowman who won nine Cups. Scotty thought so much of the Cup that he named his son, Stan Bowman, after the trophy.

S is for Stanley

It seemed unimportant; he was just being nice
in creating a prize for these wild boys on ice.
He donated the trophy that carries his name
but he never did witness a Stanley Cup game.

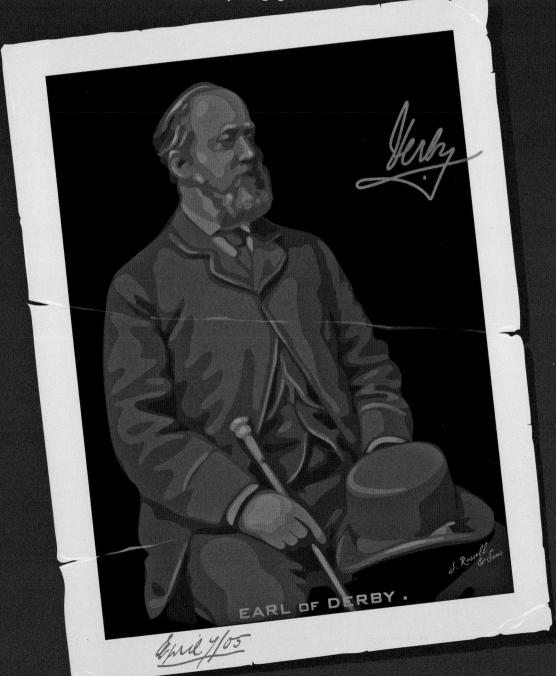

EARL OF DERBY .

Lord Frederick Arthur Stanley made his lasting gift to hockey because his family, stationed in Ottawa as representatives for Queen Victoria, so loved the game. He requested the creation of a trophy for the best amateur team in Canada. The Cup was manufactured in England and cost about $50.

As Governor General, Lord Stanley travelled extensively in Canada and also lent his name for Vancouver's Stanley Park. His time in Canada lasted only five years and he was not able to see a Stanley Cup game, let alone award the trophy that bore his name.

Tt

T is for Toronto Maple Leafs

Their season might end with some faraway team
ruining the Maple Leafs' Stanley Cup dream.
While others say *quit*, a Leafs fan says *never*;
they're true to their team forever and ever.

Conn Smythe rose from one of Toronto's poorest areas to become a varsity hockey player, entrepreneur, and war hero. When Smythe and a group of business people bought the team in 1927, he chose the name Maple Leafs to honour Canada's national symbol. The Conn Smythe Trophy is awarded every year to the most valuable player in the playoffs.

The Maple Leafs have won 13 Stanley Cups, more than any team except for the Montreal Canadiens. While the Leafs' last championship came way back in 1967, Leafs fans believe sooner or later their faith will be rewarded.

The Stanley Cup playoffs are full of stories where teams given little chance of winning have pulled off amazing victories.

In the 1937–38 season, the Chicago Blackhawks could not muster a winning regular-season record but they upset Montreal and Toronto to win the Cup. Chicago was a very low-scoring team but goalie Mike Karakas lifted them to a championship. In 1982 the Los Angeles Kings beat the Edmonton Oilers, who had twice as many regular-season wins. The Oilers would find themselves on the right end of an upset in 2006 when, as the eighth and final team in the Western Conference, they defeated the number one-seeded Detroit Red Wings.

The Nashville Predators were a wild card underdog in the 2017 Stanley Cup playoffs. After a hard-fought playoff, they lost to the Pittsburgh Penguins in six games.

U u

U is for Upsets and Underdogs

"May the best team win" is easy to say
but sometimes upsets get in the way.
One team may seem a whole lot better
but the winner is the team that comes together.

V is for Victory

No sooner do they put it down
and watch as it is passed around,
than players start thinking it would be great
to have two straight years to celebrate.

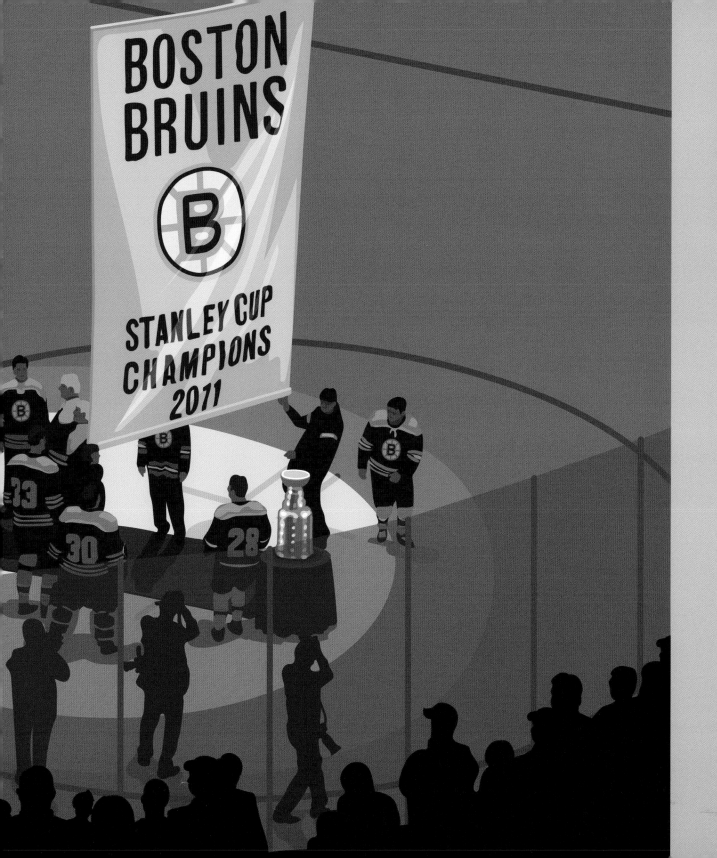

If winning the Stanley Cup is hard, winning back-to-back titles is next to impossible. With 31 teams in the NHL, the chances of winning five consecutive championships, as the Montreal Canadiens did twice, are slim. Player fatigue and injuries can be a factor. The Stanley Cup is awarded in June and those who make it to the finals play two months longer than do players from teams who did not qualify for the postseason.

W
W
W

In 1902 there was no radio or television and most Canadians did not own a phone. The Internet was still many decades in the future. So how did you find out how your team was doing in their quest for the Stanley Cup?

The best way for fans of the Toronto Wellingtons to learn of their team's challenge game in Winnipeg was to listen for a whistle blast. A few moments after the game's final whistle a Winnipeg telegraph operator transmitted the score back to a Toronto rail yard. One blast meant a Toronto win. Two told of a Winnipeg victory. When they heard the second blast Toronto fans slammed their windows in disappointment.

W is for Whistle

It didn't matter if it snowed or rained;
 they opened their windows anyway.
  But two mighty blasts from the railway yard
   brought news the fans took awfully hard.

Only one name has been X'd out on the Stanley Cup but there have been some spelling errors. The most recent one concerned Colorado Avalanche forward Adam Deadmarsh, whose name had to be fixed after "Deadmarch" appeared on the Cup.

Since 1989, Louise St. Jacques has applied the new names every year from her shop in Montreal. Technically, the Stanley Cup is not engraved. Instead, individual letters are stamped into the silver. Each name takes St. Jacques about half an hour. When Louise retires, her successor will do what each new craftsperson has done: stamp their predecessor's initials into the inside of the Cup.

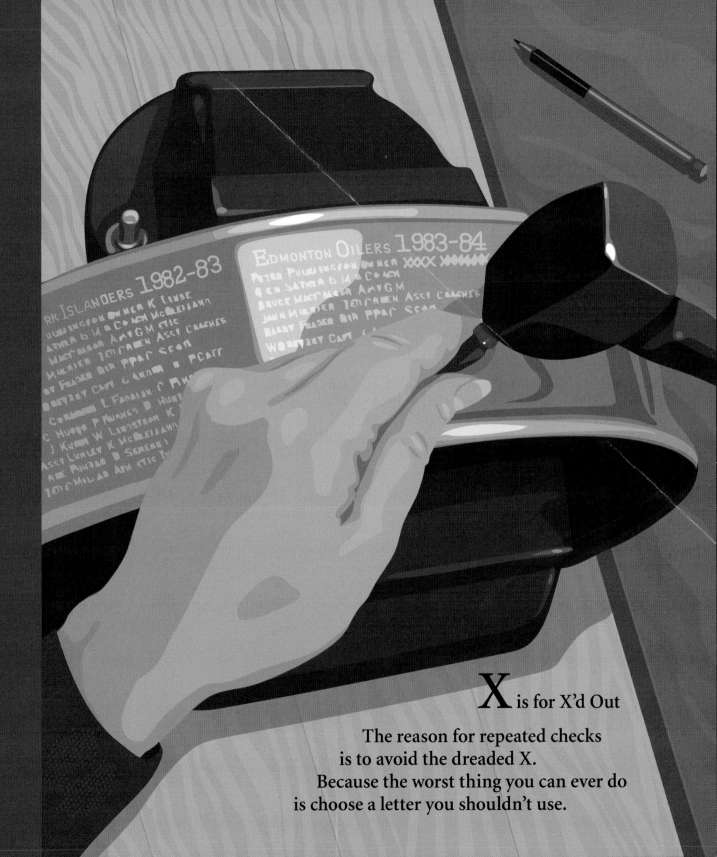

X is for X'd Out

The reason for repeated checks
is to avoid the dreaded X.
Because the worst thing you can ever do
is choose a letter you shouldn't use.

Y is for Yzerman

Of all the captains, all the kings
handed those shining, silver rings,
none stood as tall as number 19 did
when he passed the Cup to his seated friend.

When the Detroit Red Wings won their second consecutive Cup in 1998, it was clear to captain Steve Yzerman who he should give the Cup to first. A year before, defenceman Vladimir Konstantinov and trainer Sergei Mnatsakaǹov suffered terrible injuries in a car accident. Yzerman passed the Cup to the wheelchair-bound Konstantinov.

In another example of a captain's kindness, Colorado's Joe Sakic did not lift the Cup when the Avalanche won in 2001 but instead passed it to teammate Ray Bourque. It was the final night of Bourque's great 22-year career.

Z is for St. Paul's Zamboni Parade

When hockey returned to the hockey state,
the time had come for a big parade.
But without a float or a marching band,
they used what hockey states have on hand.

They had a problem in St. Paul, Minnesota, on June 25, 1997. The NHL had just awarded a new hockey team for the Twin Cities of Minneapolis and St. Paul. The region had been without an NHL team for four years. There was no arena, no coach, no players, not even a team name. So the parade celebrating the return of hockey to Minnesota was made up of Zambonis brought together from nearby arenas.

They still speak of the Zamboni parade in Minnesota, the home of the Wild. Minnesotans love the game so much their home is often called the State of Hockey.

Complete List *of* Stanley Cup Winning Teams

2017	Pittsburgh Penguins	1987	Edmonton Oilers	1958	Montreal Canadiens	1929	Boston Bruins	1908	Montreal Wanderers
2016	Pittsburgh Penguins	1986	Montreal Canadiens	1957	Montreal Canadiens	1928	New York Rangers	1907	Montreal Wanderers
2015	Chicago Blackhawks	1985	Edmonton Oilers	1956	Montreal Canadiens	1927	Ottawa Senators		Kenora Thistles
2014	Los Angeles Kings	1984	Edmonton Oilers	1955	Detroit Red Wings			1906	Montreal Wanderers
2013	Chicago Blackhawks	1983	New York Islanders	1954	Detroit Red Wings	**The NHL assumed control**			Ottawa Silver Seven
2012	Los Angeles Kings	1982	New York Islanders	1953	Montreal Canadiens	**of Stanley Cup competition**		1905	Ottawa Silver Seven
2011	Boston Bruins	1981	New York Islanders	1952	Detroit Red Wings	**after 1926**		1904	Ottawa Silver Seven
2010	Chicago Blackhawks	1980	New York Islanders	1951	Toronto Maple Leafs			1903	Ottawa Silver Seven
2009	Pittsburgh Penguins	1979	Montreal Canadiens	1950	Detroit Red Wings	1926	Montreal Maroons		Montreal AAA
2008	Detroit Red Wings	1978	Montreal Canadiens	1949	Toronto Maple Leafs	1925	Victoria Cougars	1902	Montreal AAA
2007	Anaheim Ducks	1977	Montreal Canadiens	1948	Toronto Maple Leafs	1924	Montreal Canadiens		Winnipeg Victorias
2006	Carolina Hurricanes	1976	Montreal Canadiens	1947	Toronto Maple Leafs	1923	Ottawa Senators	1901	Winnipeg Victorias
2004	Tampa Bay Lightning	1975	Philadelphia Flyers	1946	Montreal Canadiens	1922	Toronto St. Pats	1900	Montreal Shamrocks
2003	New Jersey Devils	1974	Philadelphia Flyers	1945	Toronto Maple Leafs	1921	Ottawa Senators	1899	Montreal Shamrocks
2002	Detroit Red Wings	1973	Montreal Canadiens	1944	Montreal Canadiens	1920	Ottawa Senators		Montreal Victorias
2001	Colorado Avalanche	1972	Boston Bruins	1943	Detroit Red Wings	1919	*No decision–series*	1898	Montreal Victorias
2000	New Jersey Devils	1971	Montreal Canadiens	1942	Toronto Maple Leafs		*beween Montreal and*	1897	Montreal Victorias
1999	Dallas Stars	1970	Boston Bruins	1941	Boston Bruins		*Seattle cancelled due to*	1896	Montreal Victorias
1998	Detroit Red Wings	1969	Montreal Canadiens	1940	New York Rangers		*influenza epidemic*		Winnipeg Victorias
1997	Detroit Red Wings	1968	Montreal Canadiens	1939	Boston Bruins	1918	Toronto Arenas	1895	Montreal Victorias
1996	Colorado Avalanche	1967	Toronto Maple Leafs	1938	Chicago Blackhawks	1917	Seattle Metropolitans	1894	Montreal AAA
1995	New Jersey Devils	1966	Montreal Canadiens	1937	Detroit Red Wings	1916	Montreal Canadiens	1893	Montreal AAA
1994	New York Rangers	1965	Montreal Canadiens	1936	Detroit Red Wings	1915	Vancouver Millionaires		
1993	Montreal Canadiens	1964	Toronto Maple Leafs	1935	Montreal Maroons	1914	Toronto Blueshirts		
1992	Pittsburgh Penguins	1963	Toronto Maple Leafs	1934	Chicago Blackhawks	1913	Quebec Bulldogs		
1991	Pittsburgh Penguins	1962	Toronto Maple Leafs	1933	New York Rangers	1912	Quebec Bulldogs		
1990	Edmonton Oilers	1961	Chicago Blackhawks	1932	Toronto Maple Leafs	1911	Ottawa Senators		
1989	Calgary Flames	1960	Montreal Canadiens	1931	Montreal Canadiens	1910	Montreal Wanderers		
1988	Edmonton Oilers	1959	Montreal Canadiens	1930	Montreal Canadiens	1909	Ottawa Senators		

To Connor and Gavin, my two favourite players; Pat Quinn, my all-time favourite coach; and the geriatric gentlemen of the Westdale Men's Hockey League.

—Mike

To my son, Austin, for all our knee hockey, roller hockey, and skating on the Erie Canal. I loved every game.

And to my daughter, Clare, for putting up with us!

—Chris